NEW EDITION! OVER 1 MILLION COPIES SOLD!

The Complete Guitar Player

by Russ Shipton

Book 2

Wise Publications London / New York / Paris / Sydney / Copenhagen / Madrid / Tokyo

Music Theory

So that you can understand the sheet music of any songs you want to learn and play on your guitar, you must be able to read the melody notes as they're shown on the 'treble clef'. If you don't know, or aren't sure exactly how this standard music notation works, go carefully through this page - it follows simple rules, and is easier than it looks!

The first seven letters of the alphabet are used, but the intervals between them are not the same...

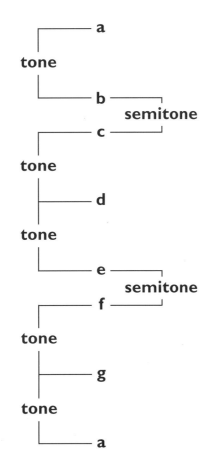

Between the notes **e** and **f** and **b** and **c**, there is no intermediary note. Between the others there is a note that's called 'sharp' or 'flat'. In other words, the note between **a** and **b** may be called **a♯** (sharp) or **b♭** (flat). Can you guess the note between **f** and **g**? Yes, that's right, **f♯** or **g♭**.

Pitch Intervals On The Guitar

Therefore the semitone is the smallest interval of pitch. On the guitar, moving from one fret to the next on the same string is moving a semitone (or from an open note to the 1st fret note of the same string). And moving towards the guitar body the pitch goes higher.

Music Notation

The top line of music in the song sheet or book you buy is the melody. Have a look at the treble clef and where you can find the notes...

This is the symbol for the treble clef.

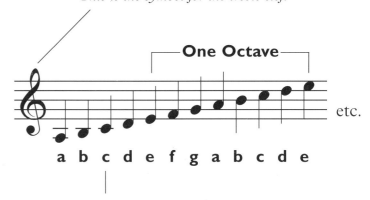

etc.

a b c d e f g a b c d e

*This is the 'middle **c**' (the **c** note in the middle of the piano). It's the 1st fret, 2nd string on the guitar, but **guitar music is shown an octave higher than actually played.***

A note is sharpened (raised by a semitone) or flattened (lowered by a semitone) with a sign placed **either** at the start of the line **or** just before it, like this...

As well as the 'pitch' (higher or lower) of the notes, the music notation tells you how long the notes last. Here are the main signs that indicate the length of time each note should last...

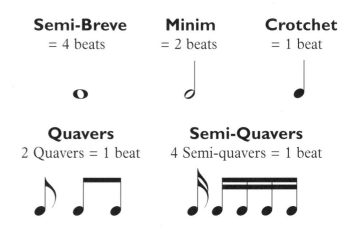

Semi-Breve = 4 beats	Minim = 2 beats	Crotchet = 1 beat

Quavers 2 Quavers = 1 beat	Semi-Quavers 4 Semi-quavers = 1 beat

More Ideas

Barre Chords

All guitarists need to learn 'barre' chords. These involve the 1st finger pressing down two or more strings. The **F** chord is an extremely important barre chord shape that requires the 1st finger to go across all six strings:

The F Chord

Drop your thumb on the neck and lean towards the end of the guitar. Adjust the 1st finger position to avoid any buzzing. To make it easier to hold the shape you could put your capo on about the 5th fret (and hold the shape on the 6th fret). Some players use their thumb for the 6th string **f** note, with a short barre across the top two or three strings:

The F Chord

The other crucial barre chord you need to learn for this book is **Bm**. Here the barre goes across at the 2nd fret. Use a capo to start with if you need to.

The Bm Chord

Finding Chord And Melody Notes

Once you've learnt the basic music theory on page 2, you'll soon be able to find and name the notes in the chords you play. You'll also be able to check the melody notes of any song you want to play and sing. For the moment you can try and commit the lower fret notes to memory.

Fill in the other notes on the diagram below. You will then see why the frets indicated are used for tuning your guitar.

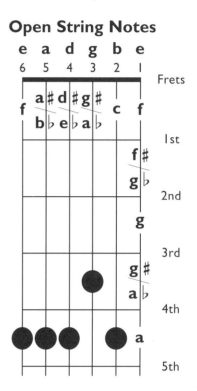

Open String Notes

One piano key to the next along = 1 semitone

One guitar fret to the next = 1 semitone

Rhythm Variations

Interesting changes to the strumming style rhythm patterns are introduced in this section. As well as learning how to swing the rhythm, you'll also be using stops and syncopation, i.e. offbeat stress.

Using A Flatpick

If you haven't yet tried using a flatpick, perhaps now is a good time to start. It will save wearing your nails down for the picking styles and allow for a greater volume range. Though it may be difficult at first to try something different, each approach will produce a particular effect and will be well worth mastering.

3

Yellow Submarine

The Beatles

Strumming Style

The swung upstrums are shown visually. It may help you to count the pattern 1, & 2, & 3, & 4, &. Play the pattern over and over, keeping the beats evenly spaced as always. The swing rhythm should feel 'jumpy'.

To start with, play 'Yellow Submarine' with swung upstrums throughout. Then try to vary the number of upstrums as shown in the accompaniment below.

Stress

Though you still emphasise the 1st beat strum, with swing strum accompaniments you should *stress every beat quite heavily.*

Melody

When you're happy with the swing rhythm accompaniment for 'Yellow Submarine', here are the first notes to help you sing the right melody:

b c d b a b g

See if you can find them on the lower frets of the guitar.

The Swing Rhythm

Most of the songs in this book are played with a 'straight' rhythm - i.e. the offbeat strums or notes are played exactly halfway between beats. Some songs, like 'Yellow Submarine', however, must be played with a swing rhythm. Delay the upstrums till just before the following beat:

4/4 Rhythm Hold any chord

Accompaniment: 4/4 Swing Rhythm

	= Strum down
	= Strum up

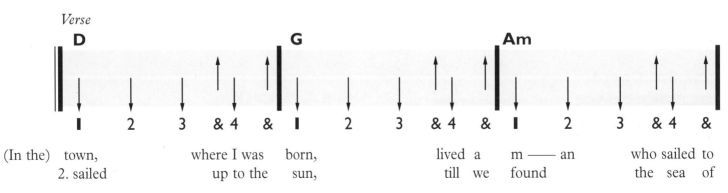

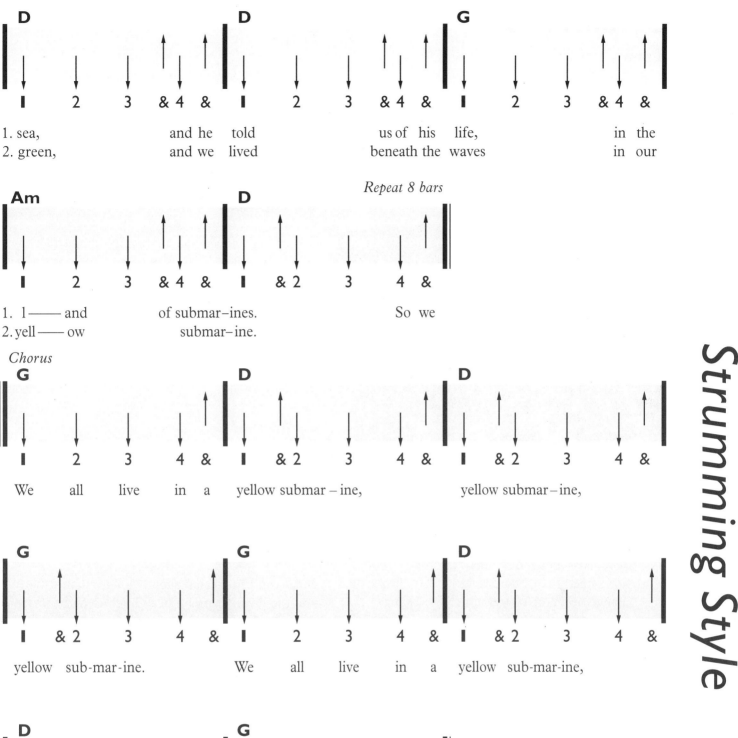

D   **D**   **G**

1   2   3   & 4 &   1   2   3   & 4 &   1   2   3   & 4 &

1. sea,   and he told   us of his life,   in the
2. green,   and we lived   beneath the waves   in our

Repeat 8 bars

Am   **D**

1   2   3   & 4 &   1   & 2   3   4 &

1. I——— and   of submar–ines.   So we
2. yell——ow   submar–ine.

Chorus

G   **D**   **D**

1   2   3   4 &   1   & 2   3   4 &   1   & 2   3   4 &

We all live in a   yellow submar – ine,   yellow submar – ine,

G   **G**   **D**

1   & 2   3   4 &   1   2   3   4 &   1   & 2   3   4 &

yellow sub-mar-ine.   We all live in a   yellow sub-mar-ine,

D   **G**

1   & 2   3 & 4 &   1   & 2   3   4 &

yellow submar-ine,   yellow submar-ine.

More Swing Songs

Revolution (The Beatles)
When I'm Sixty-Four (The Beatles)
Girl (The Beatles)
Don't Stop (Fleetwood Mac)

You Ain't Goin' Nowhere (Bob Dylan)
Slip Slidin' Away (Paul Simon)
Song Sung Blue (Neil Diamond)
Summer Holiday (Cliff Richard)
Release Me (Engelbert Humperdink)
Lucille (Kenny Rogers)
When I Need You (Leo Sayer)

American Pie

Don McLean

New G Chord Fingering

For particular songs the standard chords sometimes need to be altered slightly. The fingering may change or a note or two added. To change quickly and smoothly between the **G** and **C** chords, try this **G** chord fingering:

G Chord

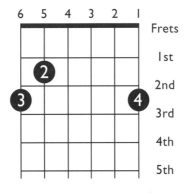

Stops

Continuous down/up strums are used for 'American Pie', apart from the stops on the **Em** chord. These help to vary the sound and improve the song dynamics. Experiment with occasional stops in songs you already know.

Syncopation

So far you've been using stress in the normal way, i.e. on the beats. If you stress an offbeat strum a little tension is created in the rhythm. This is known as 'syncopation'. One way of stressing the offbeat is to come into a chord between beats rather than on a beat. Try changing into the **D** chord *very quickly* in bars 2, 4 & 6 and striking it early, not on the 3rd beat but between beats 2 & 3. This matches the timing of the lyrics:

4/4 Rhythm

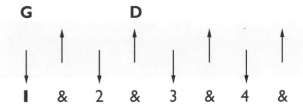

Make the **D** upstrum slightly longer than usual and the downstrum on beat 3 lighter and shorter than usual. The bar is counted the same, but the rhythmic feel is different.

The D Run

An extremely common guitar trick when holding a **D** chord for more than one bar is to remove the 2nd finger or add the 4th finger, or both. Play the last **D** bars normally to start with, then try following the indications above the notation. This produces a treble note run and stresses the offbeat notes. The movement and slight syncopation makes the accompaniment more interesting.

Melody

Here are the first notes of the chorus:

d (low) **d** (high) **c c c b a g a**

Try to find them on the lower frets of the guitar.

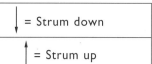

Accompaniment: 4/4 Rhythm

Chorus

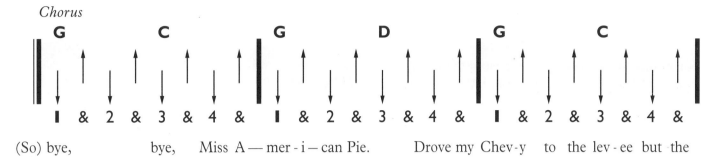

(So) bye,   bye,   Miss A — mer - i — can Pie.   Drove my Chev-y   to the lev - ee but the

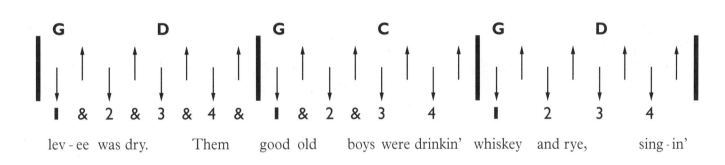

lev - ee was dry.   Them   good old   boys were drinkin' whiskey and rye,   sing - in'

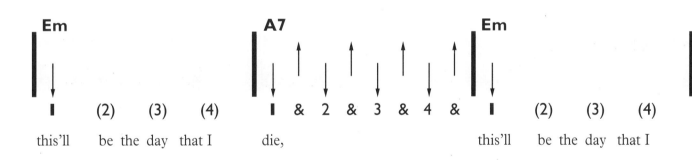

this'll   be the day that I   die,   this'll   be the day that I

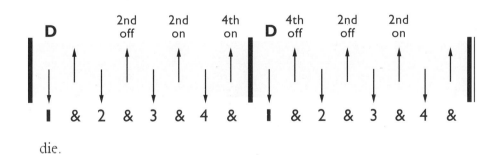

die.

Words & Music by Don McLean

© *Copyright 1971 & 1972 Mayday Music Incorporated & Benny Bird Music, USA.*
Universal/MCA Music Limited, 77 Fulham Palace Road, London W6.
All Rights Reserved. International Copyright Secured.

7

Brown Eyed Girl

Van Morrison

Strumming Style

Half Bar Stress

Sometimes an offbeat stress is part of the main rhythmic feel of an accompaniment. Van Morrison's 'Brown Eyed Girl' requires a stress between the 2nd & 3rd beats. The stress in the middle of a bar is a very common place for syncopation and is found in many areas of modern music:

4/4 Rhythm Hold any chord

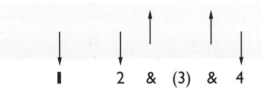

Make the upstrum between beats 2 & 3 a little longer than usual, i.e. four or five strings instead of two or three. To help you keep the rhythm you should do an 'airstroke' with your hand (or pick) on the 3rd beat. In other words move your hand downwards without touching the strings.

If you do strum on this beat it should be short and very light.

Speed

This accompaniment should be played quite fast, at about 155 beats per minute. The standard music expression for a fast tempo is 'allegro'.

The Bm Chord

The **Bm** chord is used in this arrangement. See page 3 for the fingering of this common barre chord.

Melody

String	┌3rd┐	4th	┌3rd┐	┌──4th──┐
Fret	2 0	4 0 2	4	2 0 2

Hey where did we go, days when the rains

4th	┌───3rd───┐	┌───4th───┐
4	2 2 2 2 02	4 2 0 2 4

came, down in the hollow, playin' a new game.

4th	┌────3rd────┐	┌──4th──┐
4 2	2 2 2 0 2 0	4 4 2 0

Laughin' and a-runnin', hey hey, skippin' and a-

┌4th┐	┌───3rd───┐	┌4th┐
2 2	2 2 2 2 2 0 2 0	4 0

jumpin', in the misty mornin' fog with our, our

┌─────────4th─────────┐
2 2 4   4   4   0   0   4   4   0

hearts a-thumpin', and you, my brown eyed girl.

┌2nd┐	┌──4th──┐
3 0	4 4 0

You, my brown eyed girl.

Accompaniment: 4/4 Rhythm

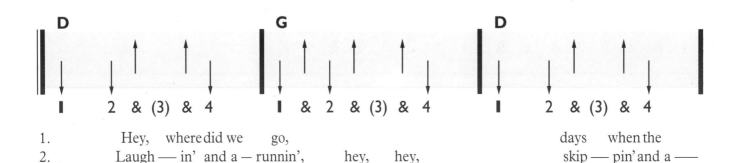

| 1. | Hey, | where did we | go, | | | days | when the |
| 2. | Laugh — in' and a – runnin', | | hey, | hey, | | skip — pin' and a — |

↓ = Strum down

↑ = Strum up

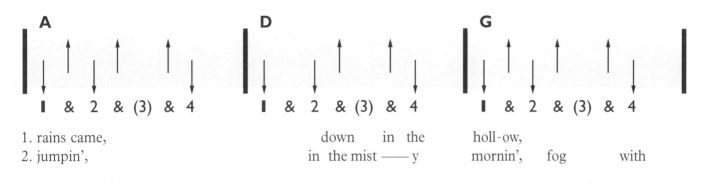

1. rains came,   down   in   the   holl-ow,
2. jumpin',   in the mist —— y   mornin', fog   with

Repeat 8 bars

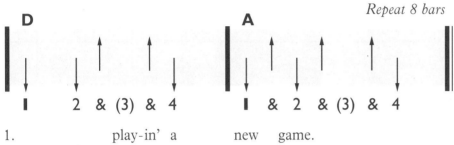

1.   play-in' a   new   game.
2.   our,   our   hearts a-thumpin',   and

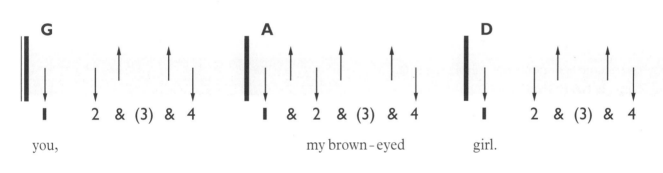

you,   my brown-eyed   girl.

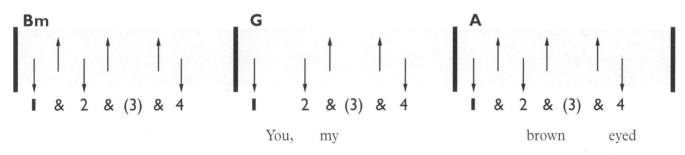

You,   my   brown   eyed

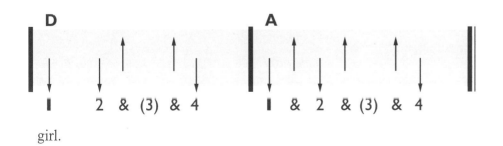

girl.

Words & Music by Van Morrison

Eternal Flame

The Bangles

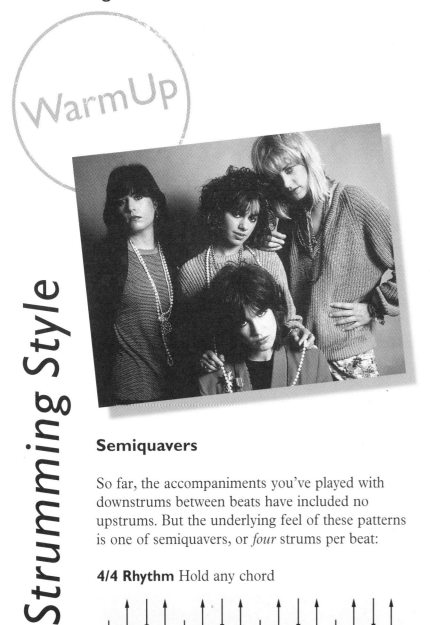

Strumming Style

Semiquavers

So far, the accompaniments you've played with downstrums between beats have included no upstrums. But the underlying feel of these patterns is one of semiquavers, or *four* strums per beat:

4/4 Rhythm Hold any chord

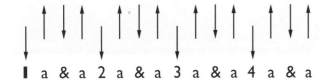

1 a & a 2 a & a 3 a & a 4 a & a

Play longer downstrums on each beat and stress each of them. Count the pattern as indicated. As with other strum patterns, you can remove some of the upstrums to produce a variety of rhythmic effects.

When you've mastered the combination I've given for the accompaniment, try some pattern variations of your own.

The F & Dm Chords

The **Bm** barre chord you played in the last accompaniment is also used in the verse of 'Eternal Flame'. You'll need to learn another common barre chord for the middle section of the song (shown at the end of the book). Together with **Bm**, the **F** chord is shown on page 3.

Another new chord you'll need to know for the middle section is **Dm**:

Dm Chord

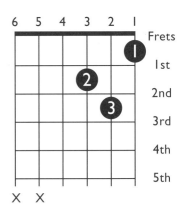

Melody

Check the melody of 'Eternal Flame' by picking out the notes shown below. Work out the note names and then try singing the melody. Male singers should find and sing the notes an octave lower.

String			2nd			1st	2nd	3rd	
Fret	0	1	3	3	3	0	3	0	2

Close your eyes, give me your hand, darling

2nd			1st				2nd
0	3	3	3	3	3	0	0	3

Do you feel my heart beating? Do you

3rd	2nd			1st					
0	2	0	3	3	2	7	7	0 2 3 0

understand? Do you feel the same? Am I only

1st		2nd			1st	2nd
5	3	3	3	3	3	3 3 2 3	3

dreaming? Is this burning an eternal flame?

Accompaniment: 4/4 Rhythm

Verse

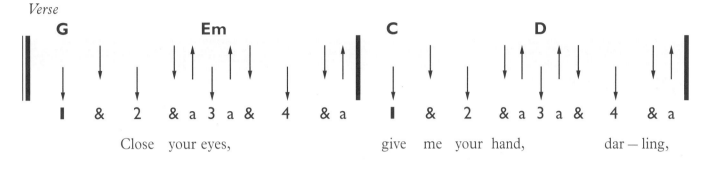

Close your eyes, give me your hand, dar — ling,

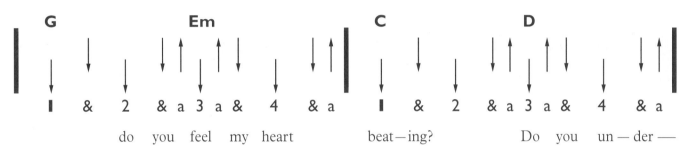

do you feel my heart beat—ing? Do you un—der —

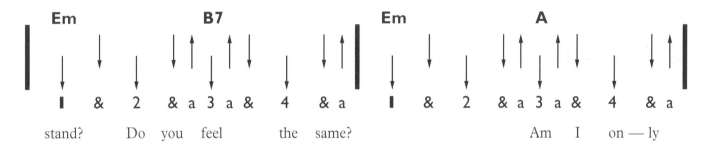

stand? Do you feel the same? Am I on — ly

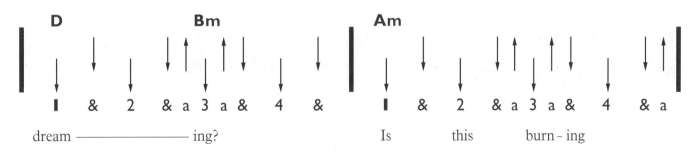

dream ————————ing? Is this burn-ing

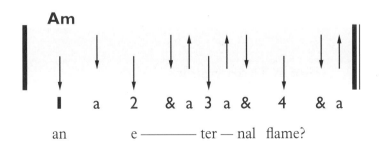

an e ———— ter — nal flame?

Words & Music by Billy Steinberg, Tom Kelly & Susanna Hoffs

More Ideas

Bass Runs

Bass runs are used to link chords and break up the usual bass-strum patterns. Try this run between the **A** and **D** chords:

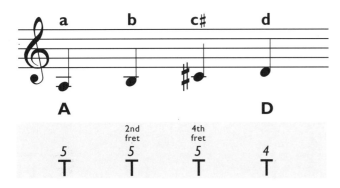

Use your 1st and 3rd fingers for the **b** & **c♯** notes. Moving back for a **D** to an **A** chord, the notes can be played in reverse. Similar runs can be used between other chords:

G to **C** = **g a b c** (on 6th & 5th strings)

D to **G** = **d e f♯ g** (for **e f♯** & **g** use 6th string)

E to **A** = **e f♯ g♯ a** (from 6th to 5th string)

C to **F** = **c d e f** (from 5th to 4th string)

Use your 2nd & 3rd fingers, except for **g♯** where the 4th finger is needed. Bass runs can also link a major and minor chord:

Am to **C** = **a b c** (5th string)

Em to **G** = **e f♯ g** (6th string)

Normally the first chord is held by the left hand until the fingers have to move to hold a fretted run note. When the final run note is played, the left hand is in the new chord position. Bass run notes have to be fitted into the 4/4 or 3/4 rhythm patterns in particular ways so they sound right. The next three songs show how this can be done.

When you've been through the accompaniments in this section, go back to the bass-strum section in Book 1 and spice up the accompaniments with some hammer-ons and bass runs.

The Hammer-on

The hammer-on is perhaps the most used of the guitar embellishments. After a first note has been sounded by the right hand striking a string, the left hand produces a second note by coming down firmly onto a higher fret. Lower string hammer-ons are easier to do and are often used to make bass-strum accompaniments more interesting. Try these examples which involve an open string with a hammer-on to the 2nd fret:

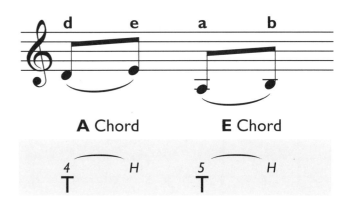

Use your 1st finger for the **E** note and 2nd finger for the **B**. Count the two notes '1 &'. Come down fast and firmly so the hammered note is clearly sounded. Now try fingering a whole **A** chord and do the same on the 4th string, then an **E** chord and do the same on the 5th string. Just raise the appropriate finger and hammer it down again.

Fretted notes of many chords will sound great when they are hammered down from an open string. Here are the chords you've learnt so far and the notes normally used for hammer-ons:

A Am A7 or **C: d** to **e** (4th string)

A Am D or **Dm: g** to **a** (3rd string)

G E Em E7 or **B7: a** to **b** (5th string)

You'll notice that these common hammer-on notes are a tone apart in pitch (two frets on the guitar).

Using A Thumbpick

If you want to make the bass notes stand out, but don't feel comfortable with a flatpick for the bass-strum style, you could try using a thumbpick. It's always worth experimenting with different approaches which can produce varied effects.

Country Waltz

Russ Shipton

$\overset{4\frown H}{T}$ = Thumb plays 4th string left hand hammers-on

↓ = Strum down

↑ = Strum up

Bass Runs And Hammer-ons In 3/4 Rhythm

This instrumental illustrates how bass runs and hammer-ons can be used in the 3/4 rhythm. Follow the fret and string numbers above the thumb indications carefully.

For the **A** to **E** bass run in bar 6 and the **A** to **D** run in bar 10, take your hand off the chord after the 1st beat and be in the new chord position for the 1st beat of the next bar. The **E** to **A** run in bar 14 involves moving the left hand after the strum on beat 2. Then use your 1st finger for the 2nd fret **f♯** note and hammer your 3rd finger down for the **g♯** on the 4th fret.

All the other hammer-ons are from an open string to the usual fretted note for the chord.

Accompaniment: 3/4 Rhythm

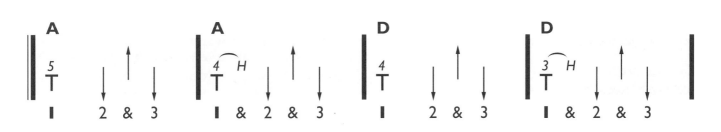

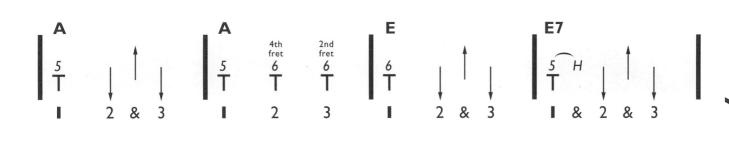

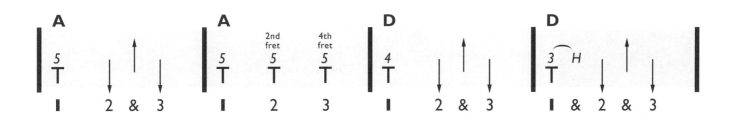

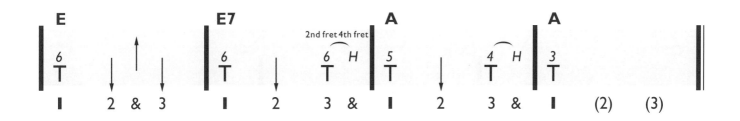

Dedicated Follower Of Fashion

The Kinks

Bass-Strum Style (vertical left margin)

More Chords

You now need to learn four new chords for this next accompaniment.

Csus4 Chord

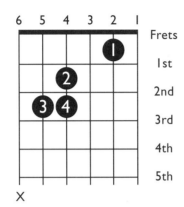

G7 Chord

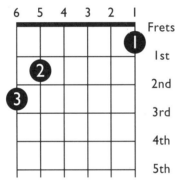

A7 Chord

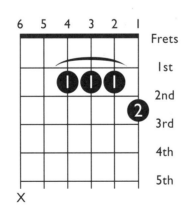

Dm7 Chord

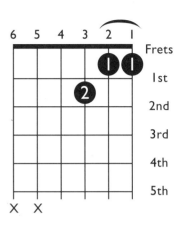

The **Csus4** means adding an **f** note temporarily to the usual **C** chord (with the 4th finger).
The **G7** is straightforward. The **A7** is another version, this time involving a short bar.
The **Dm7** (**D** minor seventh) involves adding another note to the standard minor chord. Here this means using a short bar.

Bass Runs In 4/4 Rhythm

This arrangement provides some ideas on how to fit bass runs into 4/4 bass-strum patterns. Follow the bass string and fret indications carefully and take your hand off the chord only when you need to. Be in the new chord for the last note of each run.

Lead-In

The Kinks use a strumming style lead-in, with strums on just beats 1 & 3. Tap your foot on each beat and count the rhythm carefully. After verse 1 return to bar 3 of the lead-in to begin verse 2. The chorus is given at the end of the book.

Accompaniment: 4/4 Rhythm

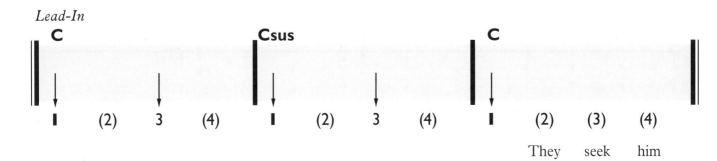

4 H T	= Thumb plays 4th string left hand hammers-on
↓	= Strum down
↑	= Strum up

Verse

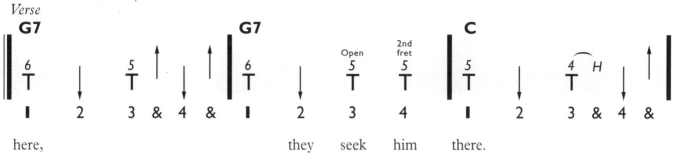

here,   they   seek   him   there.

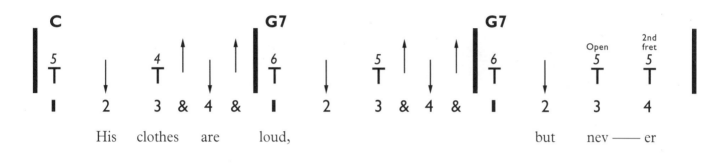

His   clothes   are   loud,   but   nev —— er

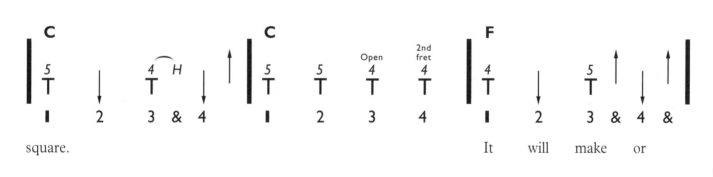

square.   It   will   make   or

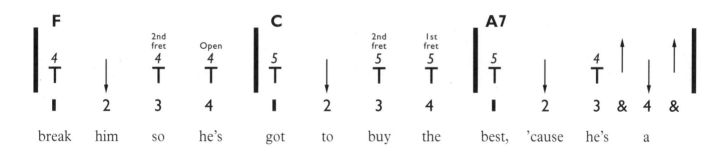

break   him   so   he's   got   to   buy   the   best,   'cause   he's   a

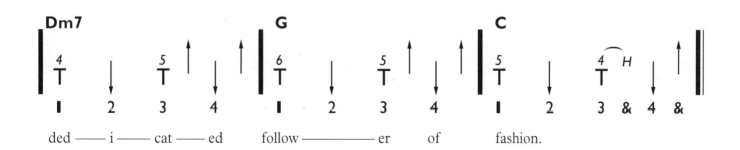

ded —— i —— cat —— ed   follow ———— er   of   fashion.

Words & Music by Ray Davies

Like A Rolling Stone

Bob Dylan

'Slow' Bass Runs

This arrangement involves rising and falling bass runs, but here the notes of the runs come on every other beat. Follow the bass string and fret indications and the **c d e** & **f** run from the 5th to 4th strings will emerge.

Pattern Changes And Repeats

Semiquaver strums are included in this accompaniment. Watch out for all the typical Dylan repetition of lines which helps to get his message over more forcefully. The last two bars shown for the chorus need to be played 5 times, the last time instrumentally after you've sung 'stone'.

Try using a flatpick instead of thumb and fingers if you want to produce a heavier sound.

Bass-Strum Style

Accompaniment: 4/4 Rhythm

Verse

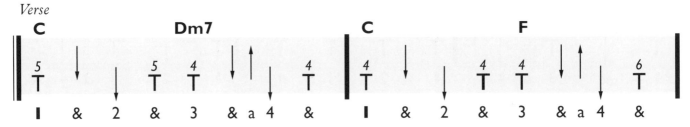

1. Once upon   a time you dressed so   fine   you   threw the bums a dime,   in your prime,
2.   people'd   call,   say 'Be — ware, doll, you're bound to fall', you thought they were   all

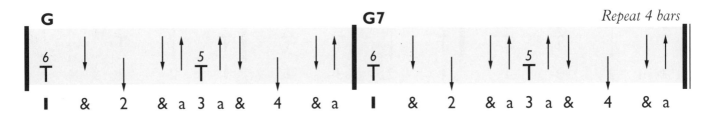

1.   didn't you?
2.   a-kiddin' you.

Chorus

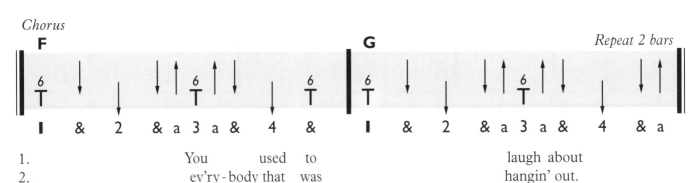

1.   You   used   to
2.   ev'ry-body that   was

1.   laugh about
2.   hangin' out.

16

Bass-Strum Style

= Thumb plays 5th string				
= Strum down				
= Strum up				

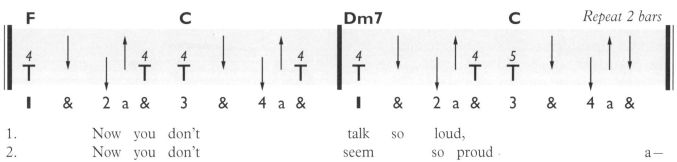

F   **C**   **Dm7**   **C**   *Repeat 2 bars*

1   &   2   a &   3   &   4   a &   1   &   2   a &   3   &   4   a &

1.   Now you don't   talk so loud,
2.   Now you don't   seem so proud   a—

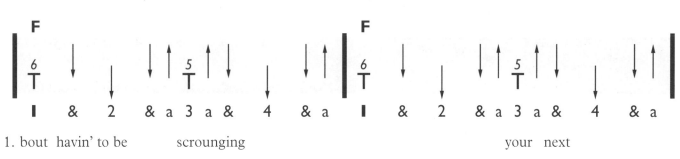

F   **F**

1   &   2   & a 3 a &   4   & a   1   &   2   & a 3 a &   4   & a

1. bout havin' to be   scrounging   your next

G   **G**

1   &   2   & a 3 a &   4   & a   1   &   2   & a 3   &   4   & a

1. meal.   How does it

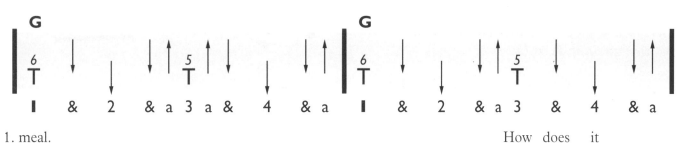

Chorus

C   **F**   **G**   *Repeat 2 bars x 4*

1   & a 2   &   3   & a 4   &   1   &   2   & a 3   & a 4 a &

1. feel,   how does it
2. feel,   to be without a
3. home   like a complete un ——
4. known,   like a rolling   stone.

More Ideas

Bass Runs

Like the bass-strum style, bass runs can be included in arpeggio patterns to make things more interesting. They can be two, three or four notes in length. Two-note runs are used in the accompaniment opposite for 'The House Of The Risin' Sun'. You could try using a three-note run linking the **Am** & **C** chords:

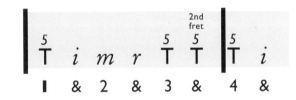

Here is an example of a four-note run in the 3/4 rhythm, from **A** to **D**:

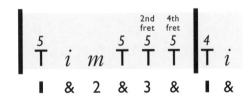

'Slow' runs can also be used in the arpeggio style, as you'll see in the arrangement for 'Sailing'. The run notes can fall on every beat (or even every other beat) instead of on and off the beat.

The 6/8 Rhythm

A number of rock, pop and blues songs are arranged with a 6/8 rhythm. The '6' means there are six beats per bar and the '8' means that each beat lasts for a quaver. This kind of rhythm is called a 'compound' rhythm because each bar is divided into two groups of three. You stress the 1st and 4th beats:

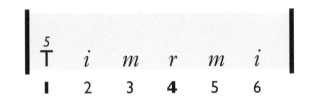

Notice the difference in stress points between the 3/4 rhythm and the 6/8 rhythm. The Animals played their version of 'The House Of The Risin' Sun' with the 6/8 rhythm, but they added a semiquaver note:

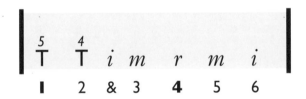

The Hammer-on

The hammer-on in the arpeggio style is usually played as a semiquaver, squeezed into a halfbeat:

The House Of The Rising Sun

Traditional, arranged by Russ Shipton

T	= Thumb
i	= Index finger
m	= Middle finger
r	= Ring finger

Accompaniment: 3/4 Rhythm

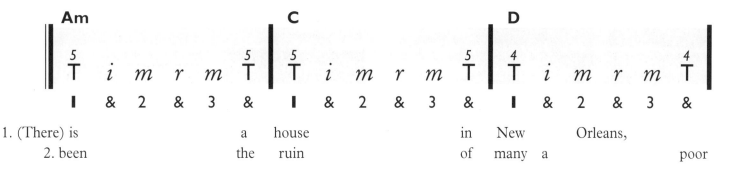

1. (There) is   a   house   in   New   Orleans,
2. been   the   ruin   of   many   a   poor

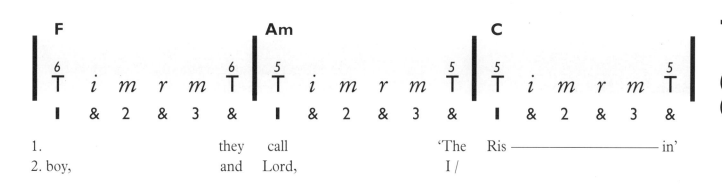

1.   they   call   'The   Ris ————————— in'
2. boy,   and   Lord,   I /

Repeat first 5 bars

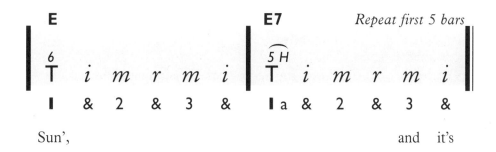

Sun',   and   it's

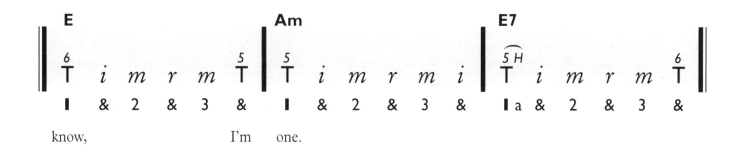

know,   I'm   one.

Sailing

Rod Stewart

Arpeggio Style

Standard Notation

This great ballad made famous by Rod Stewart involves an interesting but straightforward chord sequence in the arpeggio style. I've shown it in standard notation so you can get some practice reading the notes and finding them on the guitar.

One of the patterns you know forms the basis of the accompaniment, and there are hammer-ons (shown by small curved lines) and bass runs included to make the arrangement more interesting. All the 6th, 5th & 4th string notes are played by the right hand thumb as usual.

A New Chord

The **D** chord is sometimes replaced by the **D7** when in the key of **G** major:

D7 Chord

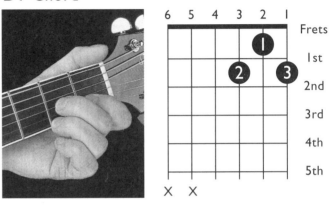

The fingering is different to the **D** chord, but just one note has changed.

In the 2nd bar of the lead-in you need to remove your 2nd finger from the top string, then put it back. This produces a treble run. The right hand thumb and all three fingers are used for the **D** chord at the end of the lead-in and for the **D7** at the end of the verse.

Melody

When you can play the accompaniment for 'Sailing', try singing as well. To help you get started, the notes for the first line are shown below. Try to find them on the lower frets.

g g b d e e

Accompaniment: 4/4 Rhythm

I am sail————ing, home a—

gain, 'cross the sea,

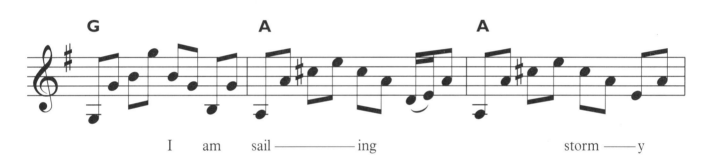

I am sail————ing storm——y

wat——ers, to be near you,

to be free.

Arpeggio Style

Words & Music by Gavin Sutherland
© Copyright 1972 Island Music Limited Universal/Island Music Limited, 77 Fulham Palace Road, London W6.
All Rights Reserved. International Copyright Secured.

Can't Help Falling In Love

Elvis Presley

6/8 Picking Patterns

Both Elvis Presley and UB40 have recorded popular versions of this song. The original was written in the 6/8 rhythm, as shown here. Stress the 1st & 4th beats and you'll produce the correct rhythmic feel for the song. Bass runs and hammer-ons are included in much the same way as in the 3/4 arpeggio patterns. Follow the string and fret indications carefully.

6/8 Strumming Patterns

Sometimes guitarists will vary an accompaniment by using a picking style for the verse and strumming for the chorus or middle section.

For the middle section of this song you could use this simple 6/8 strumming pattern:

6/8 Rhythm Finger an **Em** Chord

Make the strums on beats 1 & 4 longer and heavier.

The pattern I've given for the middle section opposite includes an upstrum between beats 5 & 6. The strum on beat 5 and the upstrum following are both semiquavers and should be played quickly. Follow the count given. When you can play the arrangement as given, you could try varying the main pattern by switching the order of the right hand fingers. You could also try adding your own hammer-ons and runs.

Other 6/8 Songs

Though the 6/8 rhythm is not as common as 4/4 and 3/4, there have been quite a few successful songs written in this rhythm. Pop hits include REM's 'Everybody Hurts', Elton John's 'I Guess That's Why They Call It The Blues', The Moody Blues' 'Nights In White Satin', 'Memory' from 'Cats', Jonathan King's 'Everyone's Gone To The Moon' and the Beatles' 'Baby's In Black'. There are many blues songs in 6/8, including Gary Moore's 'I've Still Got The Blues For You', and a number of traditional songs like 'The Mountains Of Mourne' and 'The Black Velvet Band'. Try picking or strumming a few of these songs when you can play this accompaniment.

Melody

Here are the notes for the first line. Try to find them on the lower frets:

c g c d e f e d

Accompaniment: 6/8 Rhythm

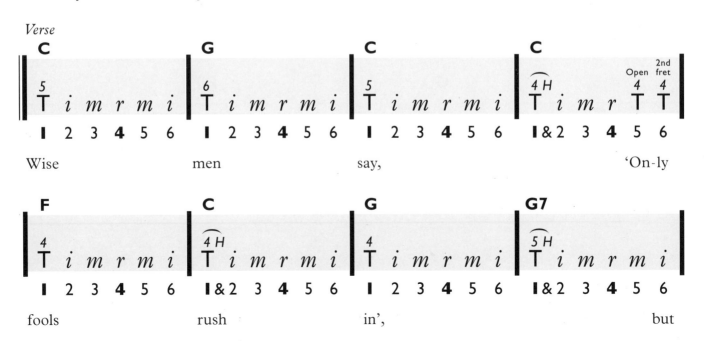

T	= Thumb
i	= Index finger
m	= Middle finger
r	= Ring finger

Arpeggio Style

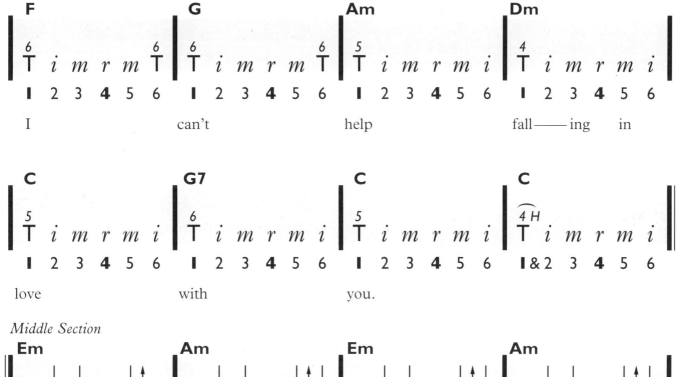

F   **G**   **Am**   **Dm**

I   can't   help   fall——ing   in

C   **G7**   **C**   **C**

love   with   you.

Middle Section

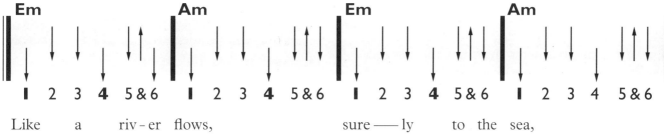

Em   **Am**   **Em**   **Am**

Like   a   riv-er flows,   sure——ly   to the sea,

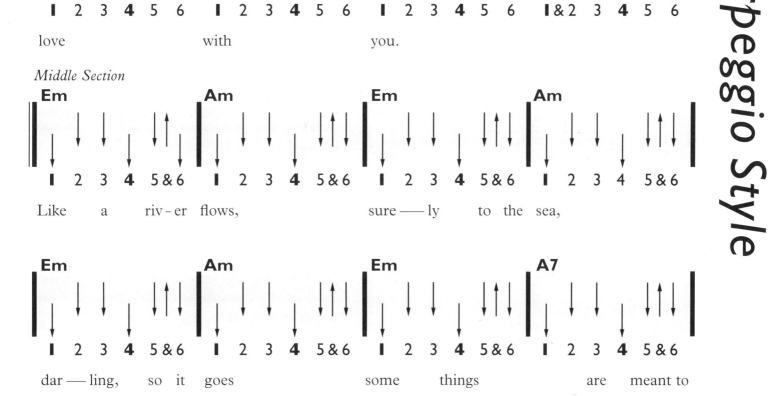

Em   **Am**   **Em**   **A7**

dar——ling,   so it goes   some   things   are   meant to

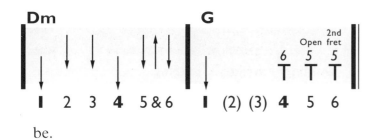

Dm   **G**

be.

Words & Music by George Weiss, Hugo Peretti & Luigi Creatore

© Copyright 1961 Gladys Music, USA.

Manor Music Company Limited, Iron Bridge House, 3 Bridge Approach, London NW1 for the United Kingdom,

Eire, Israel & the British Dominions, Colonies, Overseas Territories & Dependencies (excluding Canada, Australia and New Zealand).

All Rights Reserved. International Copyright Secured.

How To Do It

The main exponents of the alternating thumb style are folk and country pickers, like Bob Dylan, Ralph McTell and Paul Simon. There are also many blues and ragtime players who use this style, including Stefan Grossman, John Fahey, Reverend Gary Davis, Blind Blake and Mississippi John Hurt.

The essential ingredient of this style is the alternating bass part. Normally a lower bass note is followed by a higher one and the two are repeated. Hold an **E** chord and play this sequence over and over again, keeping the beats even and the speed moderate:

4/4 Rhythm Finger an **E** Chord

6	4	6	4
T	T	T	T
1	2	3	4

Don't move your right hand too much or you'll find it more difficult to strike the right string every time. While the bass notes give you a rocking and steady underlying rhythmic feel, treble notes can be added to harmonise with what you're singing. (When you become accomplished at this style, it is also possible to pick out part or the whole of a song melody, as you'll see later in the course). Try this simple pattern with just two treble notes added to the bass part:

4/4 Rhythm Finger an **E** Chord

6	4		6		4
T	T	*i*	T	*m*	T
1	2	&	3	&	4

For the moment use just two right hand fingers. *The index finger will always strike the 2nd string and the middle finger the 1st string.* Count the pattern carefully and play it quite slowly to begin with. As usual you must make sure that the beats are evenly spaced. When you have this alternating thumb pattern under control, enjoy playing 'Jolene' and 'Streets Of London'.

Simple 4/4 Pattern Sequence
Finger an **E** Chord

Thumb strikes 6th string

Thumb strikes 4th string

1st finger strikes 2nd string

Thumb strikes 6th string

2nd finger strikes 1st string

Thumb strikes 4th string

Jolene
Dolly Parton

T	= Thumb
i	= Index finger
m	= Middle finger
r	= Ring finger

Bass And Treble Variations

When you can play this accompaniment, try different bass strings for the 2nd, 3rd, and 4th beats. (Normally the 'root' note comes on the 1st beat, i.e. the note with the same name as the chord.) Also try creating new patterns by adding or removing treble notes.

Melody

The notes for the first line of the chorus are:

g a b c c d g a g e

Alternating Thumb Style

Accompaniment: 4/4 Rhythm

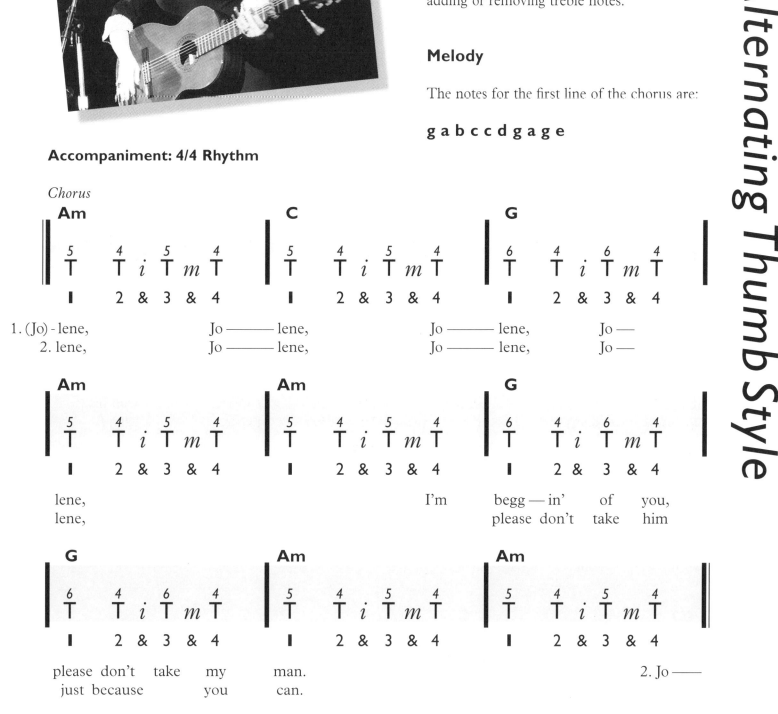

Words & Music by Dolly Parton

© Copyright 1973 Owepar Publishing Incorporated, USA.
Carlin Music Corporation, Iron Bridge House, 3 Bridge Approach, London NW1 for the British Commonwealth,
Israel and the British Dominions, Colonies, Overseas territories Dependencies (excluding Canada, Australia and New Zealand).
All Rights Reserved. International Copyright Secured.

Streets Of London

Ralph McTell

The Pinch

Ralph McTell uses the alternating thumb style for many songs. This arrangement is simpler than his, but he uses a 'pinch' at the start of his main pattern, so I've included this in each bar.

The pinch is indicated by a large 'P'. The number above it is the string to be struck by the thumb. The 1st string is played by the middle finger at the same time. The action of thumb and finger gives the pinch its name.

Different Patterns

Notice that the verse involves just one pattern and the chorus has alternating patterns. Follow the count beneath the notation carefully.

The Complete Guitar Player Tablature Book

There are many intermediate and advanced arrangements in The Complete Guitar Player Tablature Book, including Ralph McTell's original recorded version of 'Streets Of London'.

Accompaniment: 4/4 Rhythm

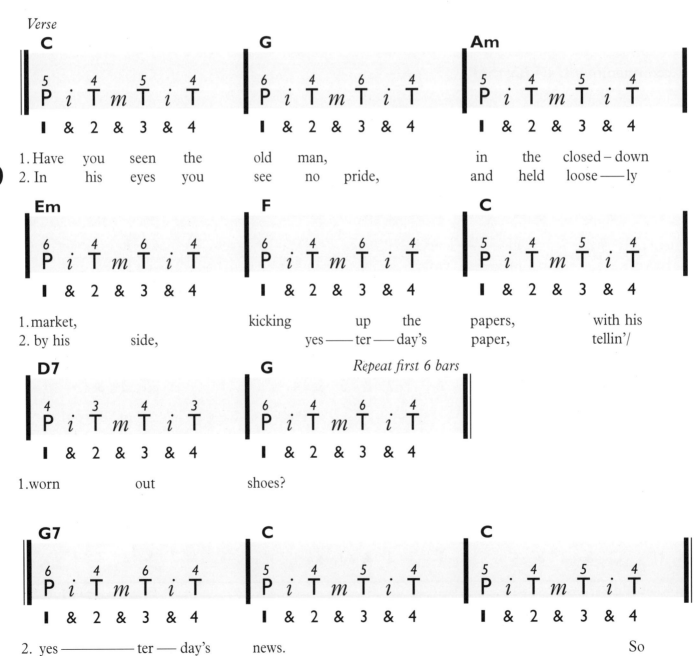

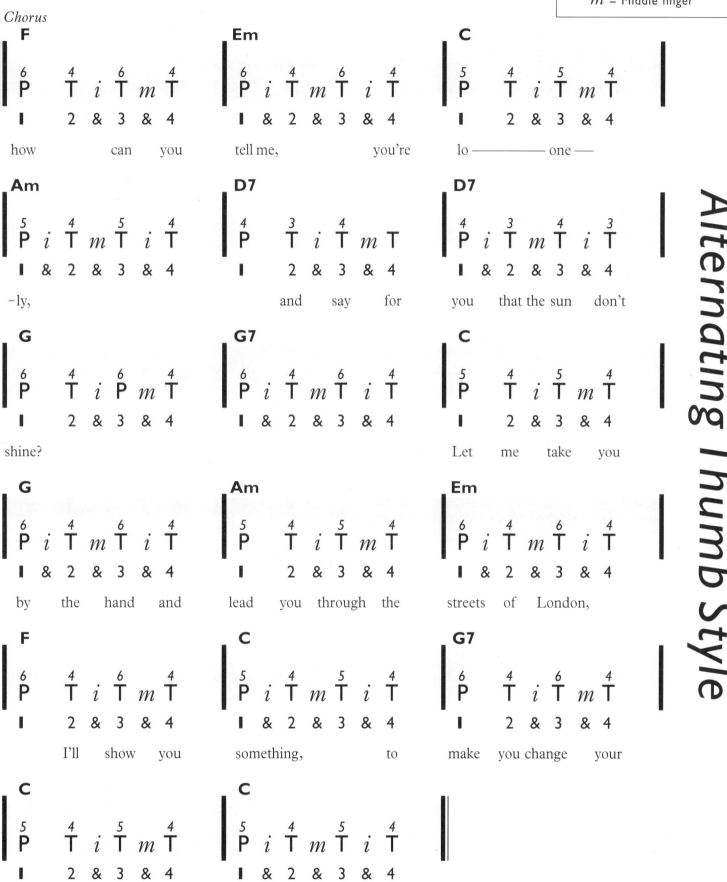

Alternating Thumb Style

Summary

Alternating Bass Notes

As mentioned on page 25, the **root** note of a chord is normally the bass note that begins an alternating thumb pattern. This is the low note that has the same name as the chord. Here are the bass strings that are most commonly played with particular chords:

E Em E7 F G and **G7** all have their root note on the 6th string. *The 6th & 4th strings are normally played for these chords,* but the 6th & 3rd might also be used. Other possibilities are: 6th 4th 5th 4th, 6th 3rd 5th 3rd, 6th 3rd 4th 3rd, or 6th 3rd 6th 4th.

A Am A7 B7 Bm and **C** all have their root note on the 5th string. *The 5th & 4th strings are normally played for these chords,* but the 5th & 3rd might also be used. Other possibilities are: 5th 4th 5th 3rd, 5th 3rd 5th 4th, 5th 4th 6th 4th or 5th 3rd 6th 3rd. The last two are only possible with the **C** chord if the 3rd finger moves to the 3rd fret of the 6th string.

D Dm Dm7 and **D7** all have their root note on the 4th string. *The 4th & 3rd strings are normally played for these chords.* Another possibility is 4th 3rd 5th 3rd.

Try changing the bass strings but for the moment use just the top two strings for the treble notes. Patterns with all three treble strings will be looked at in Book 3.

Different Patterns

Here are a number of patterns for you to play over and over until you can play them quickly and smoothly. Try using different keys and play the patterns with all the chords you know. Try working out some patterns for yourself.

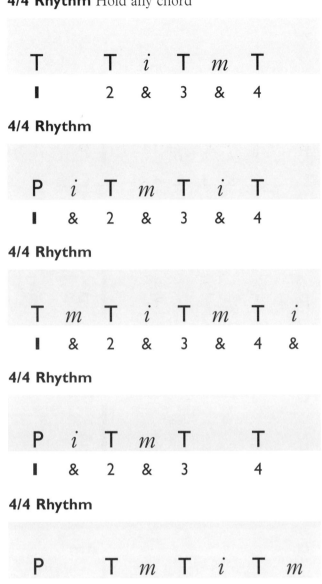

4/4 Rhythm Hold any chord

T		T	*i*	T	*m*	T
I		2	&	3	&	4

4/4 Rhythm

P	*i*	T	*m*	T	*i*	T
I	&	2	&	3	&	4

4/4 Rhythm

T	*m*	T	*i*	T	*m*	T	*i*
I	&	2	&	3	&	4	&

4/4 Rhythm

P	*i*	T	*m*	T		T	
I	&	2	&	3		4	

4/4 Rhythm

P		T	*m*	T	*i*	T	*m*
I		2	&	3	&	4	&

Other Alternating Thumb Songs

Here are some other songs that you might like to try playing with simple alternating patterns:

One Too Many Mornings (Bob Dylan)
Don't Think Twice It's All Right (Bob Dylan)
Girl Of The North Country (Bob Dylan)
Homeward Bound (Paul Simon)
April Come She Will (Paul Simon)
The Boxer (Paul Simon)
Leaves That Are Green (Paul Simon)
Ballad Of A Crystal Man (Donovan)
Four And Twenty (Stephen Stills)
Last Thing On My Mind (Tom Paxton)
Speed Of The Sound Of Loneliness (John Prine)
Castles In The Air (Don McLean)
From Clare To Here (Ralph McTell)
Life Time Lover (Jim Croce)

How To Do It

In fact, there are many different 'ways' of playing the guitar in a classical style, as there are in the other main areas of guitar music. But there's no obvious divisions like strumming, bass-strum, arpeggio and alternating thumb.

Maybe then you could say that the difference between the classical and other styles of playing is that it is more random - it doesn't stick to patterns anywhere near as much as folk or modern guitar music. There is of course another very important difference - almost always classical music is 'instrumental' only. It isn't an accompaniment for a song.

When a piece is an instrumental, it's *extremely* important to get the notes clear and to give them their full time value. It is of course very important to play all types of music well, but perhaps this classical study on the next page (and others in Book 3) will help you to concentrate on making the most of what you're playing.

Have a look at the first bar - can you remember how long the notes should last? If you've been working out or checking parts of the song melodies so far, you should know the pitch of the notes on the treble clef too...

*This means there are **4 beats** in each bar (i.e. 4 foot taps)*

This means that the length of each beat is one crotchet (4 crotchets in each bar)

Fingers

There are no hard and fast rules on which right hand finger you should use, but when two notes are played after each other on the same string, it's often a good idea for smoothness to swap fingers. I'll indicate which finger I think you should use, above each note.

As for the left hand, classical players put down only the fingers they need at the time. Other players normally use the usual whole chord shape. In fact with classical music, the emphasis is not on chords at all.

The finger that you must use for each note in this piece will be the *same as the fret number* i.e. if the note is on the 1st fret, then you must use your 1st finger, if the note's on the 2nd fret, you use your 2nd finger and so on. Only the first three frets are used in this one, so you'll only have to use your first three left hand fingers.

Finding The Notes On The Guitar

As you've been doing when finding and playing the melody notes of the songs, look for the lowest position for each note. In fact, in this piece, the 3rd fret is the highest that you go, so they'll be quite easy to find!

In the classical style the thumb must be kept clear of the fingers.

Study

Fernando Sor

Reading The Notes

Your first classical piece, a study by a famous composer and guitarist of the early 19th century, is shown in standard notation. Take each separately to start with and make sure you find the right fret for each note.

All the notes should be played at the lowest fret possible. Many notes can be played with an open string. The timing is quite easy: four beats to a bar and just minims (two beats) and crotchets (one beat) throughout.

Fingering

The fingering for the right hand is shown above the notation. The left hand fingering is straightforward. Use the 1st finger for the 1st fret notes, the 2nd finger for the 2nd fret notes and the 3rd finger for the 3rd fret notes.

Note Length

Try to make each note last as long as the music says it should last. In other words, don't take your finger off as soon as you've played the note. It's often better to leave one finger where it is until the next has been played. The sound can then be much smoother.

T = Thumb	
i = Index finger	
m = Middle finger	
r = Ring finger	

Instrumental: 4/4 Rhythm

Section One

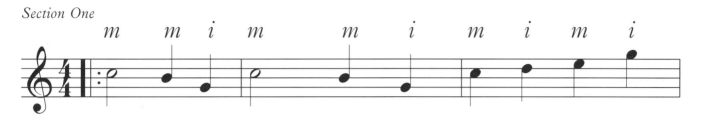

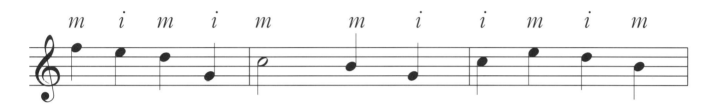

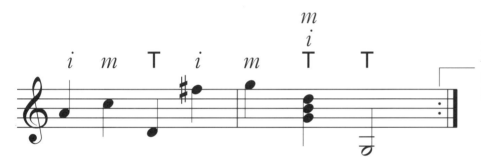

This sign means 'repeat'. In this case you go back to the start and play all 8 bars of section 1 again.

Section Two

Repeat Section Two

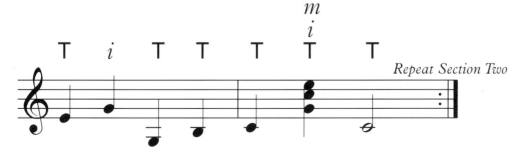

By Fernando Sor

The Major Scale

Before going on to Book 3, I'd like you to think about the Do Re Mi etc. that you've all sung at one time or another. It's the major scale that you're singing, but which one depends on which note is the starting note. All major scales sound similar in an overall way because the spaces or intervals between the notes are always the same. Let's have a look at the **C** major scale - that's the one where we don't have to bother with flats or sharps...

The C Major Scale

c d e f g a b c

To play this scale on your guitar, start by putting your 3rd finger on the left hand on the 3rd fret of the 5th string. Alternate the first two right hand fingers (don't bother with the thumb for this exercise), and use the usual left hand fingers on the appropriate frets.

When you've worked out where the notes are for the left hand, and you've played the **C** scale smoothly through a couple of times, can you work out which notes from this scale are used for the **C** chord (or **C** major chord, to give its full name)? Also, what *are* the intervals between the notes of a major scale (that are always the same)? And what's the total interval in both frets and tones between the low **c** and high **c** notes?

Now see if you can write out the **G** major scale in the same way as I've written the **C** scale above. If you keep the intervals between the notes in the same order, you should find one note that has to be 'sharpened' i.e. raised in pitch by a semitone, or fret. And then can you play it on the guitar?

These scales are extremely important because the chords and melody notes you've been playing come from scales. Try to remember the intervals of the major scale before the next book.

Useful Information

The C Major Scale

c note (low) / **d** note (open 4th string)

e note

f note / **g** note (open 3rd string)

a note / **b** note (open 2nd string)

c note (high)

Yellow Submarine

Verse 1
In the town where I was born
Lived a man who sailed to sea
And he told us of his life
In the land of submarines.

Verse 2
So we sailed up to the sun
Till we found a sea of green
And we lived beneath the waves
In our yellow submarine.

Chorus
We all live in a yellow submarine
Yellow submarine
Yellow submarine.
We all live in a yellow submarine
Yellow submarine
Yellow submarine.

Verse 3
And our friends are all aboard
Many more of them live next door
And the band begins to play...

Verse 4
As we live a life of ease
Every one of us has all we need
Sky of blue, sea of green
In our yellow submarine.

Lyrics

Lyrics

American Pie

Verse 1 (ad lib rhythm)
  G D Em   Am   C
A long, long time ago, I can still remember
             Em   **D**
how that music used to make me smile
  G   **D**   **Em**
And I knew if I had my chance
    Am   **C**
that I could make those people dance
    Em   **C**   **D**
and maybe they'd be happy for a while

Em   **Am**
But February made me shiver
Em   **Am**
  with every paper I'd deliver
C   **G**   **Am**
Bad news on the doorstep
     C   **D**
  I couldn't take one more step
G   **D**   **Em**
I can't remember if I cried
   Am   **D**
  when I read about his widowed bride
  G   **D**   **Em**
But something touched me deep inside
    C   **D** **G**
  the day the music died.

Chorus
So bye, bye, Miss American Pie
Drove my Chevy to the levee but the levee was dry
Them good old boys were drinkin' whiskey and rye
Singin' this'll be the day that I die
This'll be the day that I die.

Verse 2
  G   **Am**
  Did you write the book of love
         C   **Am**
  and do you have faith in God above
Em   **D**
  if the bible tells you so?
      G   **D**   **Em**
Now do you believe in rock and roll,
    Am   **C**
  can music save your mortal soul?
     Em   **A7**   **D**
And can you teach me how to dance real slow?
     Em   **D**
Well I know that you're in love with him,
      Em   **D**
  'cause I saw you dancin' in the gym
  C   **G**   **A7**
You both kicked off your shoes,
      C   **D**
  man I dig those rhythm and blues
    G   **D**   **Em**
I was a lonely, teenage broncin' buck
     Am   **C**
  with a pink carnation and a pickup truck
  G   **D**   **Em**   **C**   **D G C G**
But I knew I was out of luck the day the music died,
      D
I started singin'...

Verse 3
Now for ten years we've been on our own
  and moss grows fat on a rollin' stone
But that's not how it used to be
  when the jester sang for the king and queen
In a coat he borrowed from James Dean
  and a voice that came from you and me
Oh and while the king was looking down
  the jester stole his thorny crown
The courtroom was adjourned
  no verdict was returned
And while Lennon read a book on Marx
  the quartet practised in the park
And we sang dirges in the dark
We were singin'...

Verse 4

Helter-skelter in the summer swelter
    the Byrds flew off with a fallout shelter
Eight miles high and fallin' fast
    it landed foul on the grass
The players tried for a forward pass
    with a jester on the sidelines in a cast
Now the halftime air was sweet perfume while the
    sergeants played a marching tune
We all got up to dance
    but we never got the chance
'Cause the players tried to take the field
    the marching band refused to yield
Do you recall what was revealed
    the day the music died?
We started singin'...

Verse 5

And there we were all in one place
    a generation lost in space
With no time left to start again
So come on, Jack be nimble, Jack be quick
    Jack Flash sat on a candlestick
'Cause fire is the devil's only friend
And as I watched him on the stage
    my hands were clenched in fists of rage
No angel born in hell
    could break that Satan's spell
And as the flames climbed high into the night
    to light the sacrificial rite
I saw Satan laughing with delight
    the day the music died
He was singin'...

Verse 6 (ad lib rhythm, as Verse 1)

I met a girl who sang the blues
    and I asked her for some happy news
But she just smiled and turned away
I went down to the sacred store
    where I heard the music years before
But the man there said the music wouldn't play
And in the streets the children screamed
    the lovers cried and the poets dreamed
But not a word was spoken
    the church bells all were broken
And the three men I admire most
    the Father, Son and the Holy Ghost
They caught the last train for the coast
    the day the music died
And they were singin'...

Brown Eyed Girl

Verse 1

Hey where did we go, days when the rains came
Down in the hollow, playin' a new game
Laughing and a-running, hey hey
    skipping and a-jumping
In the misty morning fog with our
Our hearts a-thumping and you
My brown eyed girl
You, my brown eyed girl.

Verse 2

Whatever happened to Tuesday and so slow
Going down the old mine with a transistor radio
Standing in the sunlight, laughing
    hiding behind a rainbow's wall
Slipping and a-sliding all along
    the waterfall with you
My brown eyed girl
You, my brown eyed girl.

Middle Section

D	D	D	G

Do you remember when we used to sing

	C	G	D	G

'Sha la la, la la la la, la la la la te da

	C	G	D	G

Sha la la, la la la la, la la la la te da, la te da.

Verse 3

So hard to find my way, now that I'm all on my own
I saw you just the other day, my, how you have grown
Cast my memory back there, Lord, sometimes
    I'm overcome just thinking 'bout it
Makin' love in the green grass
    behind the stadium with you
My brown eyed girl
You, my brown eyed girl.

Eternal Flame

Verse 1
Close your eyes, give me your hand, darling
Do you feel my heart beating?
Do you understand?
Do you feel the same, am I only dreaming
Is this burning an eternal flame?

Verse 2
I believe it's meant to be, darling
I watch you when you are sleeping
You belong with me
Do you feel the same?
Am I only dreaming
Or is this burning an eternal flame?

Middle section
D   Dm G   D
Say my name, sun shines through the rain
            F   G
A whole life so lonely and then
    C   Am
Come and ease the pain
D   Bm   F C D
I don't wanna lose this feeling, oh.

Em B7 Em A7

Dedicated Follower Of Fashion

Verse 1
They seek him here, they seek him there
His clothes are loud, but never square
It will make or break him so he's got to buy the best
'Cause he's a dedicated follower of fashion.

Verse 2
And when he does his little rounds
Round the boutiques of London Town
Eagerly pursuing all the latest fads and trends
'Cause he's a dedicated follower of fashion.

Chorus
C   G G7   C
Oh yes he is, oh yes he is
              F   F   C
He thinks he is a flower to be looked at
          F   F
And when he pulls his frilly nylon
      C   *(run)*   A7
   panties right up tight,
          Dm7   G7   C
He feels a dedicated follower of fashion.

Chorus (2)
Oh yes he is, oh yes he is
There's one thing that he loves and that is flattery
One week he's in polka dots
        the next week he's in stripes
'Cause he's a dedicated follower of fashion.

Verse 3
They seek him here, they seek him there
In Regent Street and Leicester Square
Everywhere the Carnabytion Army marches on
Each one a dedicated follower of fashion.

Chorus (3)
Oh yes he is, oh yes he is
His world is built round discotheques and parties
This pleasure seeking individual always looks his best
'Cause he's a dedicated follower of fashion.

Chorus (4)
Oh yes he is, oh yes he is
He flits from shop to shop just like a butterfly
In matters of the cloth he is as fickle as can be
'Cause he's a dedicated follower of fashion.

Like A Rolling Stone

Verse 1
Once upon a time you dressed so fine
You threw the bums a dime, in your prime
Didn't you?
People'd call, say 'Beware doll, you're bound to fall'
You thought they were all kiddin' you
You used to laugh about everybody that was
    hangin' out
Now you don't talk so loud
Now you don't seem so proud
About having to be scrounging
For your next meal.

Chorus
How does it feel
How does it feel
To be without a home
Like a complete unknown
Like a rolling stone?

Verse 2
You've gone to the finest school all right
Miss Lonely, but you know you only used to get
Juiced in it
And nobody's ever taught you how to live out on
    the street
And now you're gonna have to get used to it
You said you'd never compromise
With the mystery tramp, but now you realise
He's not selling any alibis
As you stare into the vacuum of his eyes
And say
'Do you want to make a deal?'

Chorus 2
How does it feel
How does it feel
To be on your own
With no direction home
Like a complete unknown
Like a rolling stone?

Verse 3
You never turned around to see the frowns
    on the jugglers and the clowns
When they all did tricks for you
You never understood that it ain't no good
You shouldn't let other people get your kicks for you
You used to ride on the chrome horse with your
    diplomat
Who carried on his shoulder a Siamese cat
Ain't it hard when you discovered that
He really wasn't where it's at
After he took from you everything he could steal?

Verse 4
Princess on the steeple and all the pretty
    people they are drinkin'
Thinkin', that they got it made
Exchanging all precious gifts and things
But you'd better take your diamond ring
You'd better pawn it babe
You used to be so amused at Napoleon in rags
And the language that he used
Go to him now, he calls you, you can't refuse
When you got nothing, you got nothing to lose
You're invisible now
You got no secrets to conceal.

The House Of The Rising Sun

Verse 1
There is a house in New Orleans
They call 'The Risin' Sun'
And it's been the ruin of many a poor boy
And God, I know, I'm one.

Verse 2
My mother was a tailor
Sewed my new blue jeans
My father was a gamblin' man
Down in New Orleans.

Verse 3
Now the only thing to gamblin'
Is a suitcase and a trunk
And the only time he's satisfied
Is when he's on a drunk.

Verse 4
Go tell my baby sister
Not to do what I have done
To shun that house in New Orleans
They call 'The Risin' Sun'.

Verse 5
One foot on the platform
The other's on the train
I'm goin' back to New Orleans
To wear that ball and chain.

Sailing

Verse 1
I am sailing, I am sailing
Home again 'cross the sea
I am sailing stormy waters
To be near you, to be free.

Verse 2
I am flying, I am flying
Like a bird 'cross the sky
I am flying, passing high clouds
To be near you, to be free.

Verse 3
Can you hear me, can you hear me
Through the dark night, far away?
I am dying, forever crying
To be with you, who can say?

Verse 4
Can you hear me, can you hear me
Through the dark night, far away?
I am dying, forever crying
To be with you, who can say?

Verse 5
We are sailing, we are sailing
Home again 'cross the sea
We are sailing stormy waters
To be near you, to be free.

Can't Help Falling In Love

Verse 1
Wise men say
'Only fools rush in'
But I can't help
Falling in love with you.

Verse 2
Shall I stay
Would it be a sin
If I can't help
Falling in love with you?

Middle Section
Like a river flows
Surely to the sea
Darling, so it goes
Some things are meant to be.

Verse 3
Take my hand
Take my whole life too
For I can't help
Falling in love with you.

Jolene

Chorus
Jolene, Jolene, Jolene, Jolene
I'm beggin' of you, please don't take my man
Jolene, Jolene, Jolene, Jolene
Please don't take him just because you can.

Verse 1
     Am   **C**
Your beauty is beyond compare
       G   **Am**
With flaming locks of auburn hair
    G   **G**   **Am Am**
With ivory skin and eyes of emerald green
    Am   **C**
Your smile is like a breath of spring
    G   **Am**
Your voice is soft like summer rain
    G   **G**   **Am Am**
And I cannot compete with you, Jolene.

Verse 2
He talks about you in his sleep
And there's nothing I can do to keep
From crying when he calls your name, Jolene
And I can easily understand
You could easily take my man
But you don't know what he means to me, Jolene.

Verse 3
You could have your choice of men
But I could never love again
He's the only one for me, Jolene
I had to have this talk with you
My happiness depends on you
And whatever you decide to do, Jolene.

Streets Of London

Verse 1
Have you seen the old man in the closed down market
Kicking up the papers, with his worn out shoes?
In his eyes you see no pride and held loosely at his side
Yesterday's paper tellin' yesterday's news.

Chorus
So how can you tell me you're lonely
And say for you that the sun don't shine?
Let me take you by the hand and lead you through
    the streets of London
I'll show you something to make you change
    your mind.

Verse 2
Have you seen the old girl who walks the streets
    of London
Dirt in her hair and her clothes in rags?
She's no time for talkin', she just keeps right on walkin'
Carrying her home in two carrier bags.

Verse 3
In the all night cafe at a quarter past eleven
Same old man sitting there on his own
Lookin' at the world over the rim of his tea-cup
Each tea lasts an hour, and he wanders home alone.

Verse 4
Have you seen the old man outside the
    Seaman's Mission?
Memory fading with the medal ribbons that
    he wears
In our winter city, the rain cries a little pity
For one more forgotten hero and a world that
    doesn't care.

Closing Comments

Playing

Well done! You've persevered and are now becoming a versatile player. There are more advanced things coming up in Book 3, but if you've understood everything so far, you'll be able to handle the new ideas.

If you're still making buzzing noises because your fingers aren't positioned correctly, or if you still can't change chords smoothly, now is the time to do something about it. If your strings are in tune and the notes of the chords ring out clearly, your performance will sound much better!

Singing

Two things are particularly important for your singing. Firstly, the pitch of the melody notes shouldn't be out of your vocal range. Make sure you can project the lowest notes and don't worry too much about the highest notes - forcing them a little will sound fine with modern songs.

Try different capo positions to discover which key is right for each song. Secondly, breathe in the natural pauses of a song at the end of lines or phrases. Don't just breathe anywhere or you won't be able to put the words over forcefully.

Songs

It's always a great feeling to discover things yourself and do your own arranging. You've got plenty of styles and patterns now, so try them out on new songs that you can find.

Listening

Always listen to what you and others are playing. The first step is to listen carefully to the notes when you tune your guitar each day. Then listen to the sounds you're actually making when you're playing the songs you know. Finally, listen to those around you, and of course the professional guitarists' recording and live performances. See if you can recognise any of the styles you've learnt so far!

See you in Book 3 for yet more great songs and ideas...

Exclusive distributors:
Music Sales Limited
8/9 Frith Street, London WID 3JB, England.
Music Sales Pty Limited
120 Rothschild Avenue, Rosebery, NSW 2018, Australia.

Order No. AM953172 (Book & CD edition).
Order No. AM964172 (Book only).
This book © Copyright 2000 by Wise Publications.

Written and arranged by Russ Shipton.
Edited by Sorcha Armstrong.
Cover and book design by Michael Bell Design.
Cover and guitar photography by George Taylor.
Guitars supplied by Rhodes Music.
Artist photographs courtesy of
    London Features International, Retna and
    The Lebrecht Collection.
Music processed by Paul Ewers Music Design.
Printed in the United Kingdom by
    Caligraving Limited, Thetford, Norfolk.

CD programmed by John Moores.
All guitars by Arthur Dick.
Engineered by Kester Sims.

Your guarantee of quality:
As publishers, we strive to produce every book
to the highest commercial standards.
The music has been freshly engraved and the book
has carefully designed to minimise awkward page turns
and to make playing from it a real pleasure.
Particular care has been given to specifying
acid-free, neutral-sized paper made from pulps
which have not been elemental chlorine bleached.
This pulp is from farmed sustainable forests and
was produced with special regard for the environment.
Throughout, the printing and binding have been
planned to ensure a sturdy, attractive publication
which should give years of enjoyment.
If your copy fails to meet our high standards, please
inform us and we will gladly replace it.

Music Sales' complete catalogue describes
thousands of titles and is available in full colour
sections by subject, direct from Music Sales Limited.
Please state your areas of interest and send a
cheque/postal order for £1.50 for postage to:
Music Sales Limited, Newmarket Road, Bury St. Edmunds,
Suffolk IP33 3YB.

www.musicsales.com

10/03 (49081)